Mar

Classroom Questions

A SCENE BY SCENE TEACHING GUIDE

Amy Farrell

SCENE BY SCENE
ENNISKERRY, IRELAND

Scene by Scene
11 Millfield, Enniskerry
Wicklow, Ireland.
www.scenebysceneguides.com

Martyn Pig Classroom Questions/Amy Farrell. —1st ed.
ISBN 978-1-910949-24-5

Contents

Chapter One, Wednesday

Questions

1. What does Martyn tell us about his name?

2. How long ago did Martyn's story happen?

3. What is Martyn's home like?

4. What is Martyn's dad like?

5. What is Martyn's aunt like?

6. What does Martyn buy to prepare for Christmas?
    In your opinion, how does Martyn feel about Alex? Quote
    to help explain your answer.

7. When did he first meet Alex?

8.   "Now, after Alex had left on the bus, I trudged across the road feeling even worse than I'd felt before."
       Why does he feel bad?

9.   Describe Dean.

10.   Why is there shaving foam all over the kitchen window when Martyn gets home?

11.   "Of course I hated him." Do you understand why Martyn feels this way about his father?

12.   What does Alex tell Martyn about her background?

13.   Are Alex and Martyn good friends, in your opinion?

14.   "Dad was drunk when I went downstairs, which was no surprise." Does Martyn's father have a serious problem with alcohol?

15.   Do you feel sorry for Martyn when you read about what it's like for him living with his dad?

16.   'SHUT UP!' Why does Martyn get so annoyed with his father on this occasion?

17.   How does his father react?

18.   "I knew he was dead." Is this Martyn's fault?

19.   "Why didn't I try to save his life?" Why doesn't Martyn do anything here, in your opinion?

20. Do you think Alex was right not to call the police?
Is she being a good friend here?

21. "I went upstairs and got into bed." Could you do this in
Martyn's position?

Chapter Two, Thursday

Questions

1. What was Martyn's nightmare about?

2. "I couldn't get back to sleep…" Are you surprised that Martyn has trouble sleeping?

3. "What happened next, I suppose you'd call it fate." What interesting news does the postman bring?

4. How does Martyn react to this news?

5. Describe Martyn's Dad's bedroom.

6. Do you feel sorry for Martyn at this point?

7. "And how am I going to explain why it took me so long to report it?"
    Is Martyn right to worry about this?
    Is he coping with the situation, in your opinion?

8. "…all we have to do is get rid of the body…"
    Are you shocked by Martyn here?

9.   "I was just looking out for myself, that's all."
Do you agree with Martyn here, or do you think he's in the wrong?

10.   Why does Alex change her mind about telling the police?

11.   What does Martyn plan to do with the body?

12.   What part does Alex have in his plan?

13.   "She was scared of Dean. We were still in this together."
Why has Dean called around?

14.   "I know that nothing matters. That's what makes me strong."
Is Martyn a normal teenager, in your opinion?

15.   Do you think Martyn is clever, based on this chapter?

Chapter Three, Friday

Questions

1.   "We carried, we dragged, we pushed, we shoved, until eventually we got him into his bedroom and laid him out on the bed."
Could you do this or would you find it too disgusting or upsetting?

2.   "Are we bad?" Alex is worried that what she's doing is wrong. Are they bad people, in your opinion?

3.   "I wondered what Alex was thinking about." Describe their relationship.

4.   How does Alex help Martyn get ready for Aunty Jean's visit?

5.   "Unless she's lost her sense of smell she's bound to notice that stink."
Is this a gruesome scene in your opinion? Explain your point of view.

6.   What does Martyn do to cover up the fact that his father is dead?

7.   How does Alex react after they get his dad ready?
     Is this a normal reaction, in your opinion?

8.   Is Aunty Jean as bad as Martyn made out?

9.   "Aunty Jean stopped a few feet away, a look of surprise on her face."
     What different things does Aunty Jean notice that almost get Martyn caught?

10. Are you surprised that she doesn't realise what's going on?

11. What details do you learn about William from Aunty Jean?

12. How did Alex avoid being seen by Aunty Jean?

13. "It was my money." Why is the money so important to Martyn?

Chapter Four, Saturday

Questions

1. Why does Martyn decide to go to the beach?

2. "My eyes sprang open and I jerked to my feet."
    What does Martyn imagine he sees at the beach?
    Do you think he has been traumatised by what he's been
    through?

3. What do Martyn and Alex do to get his dad ready before
    they move him?

4. "Carefully, I lodged some of Dean's hairs under one of
    Dad's fingernails, wrapping the long ends round the tip of
    the finger to help keep them in place."
    Why does Martyn do this?

5. "I stared down at the big green nylon cocoon and
    wondered if I ought to feel something. Anything."
    Are you surprised that Martyn doesn't care about
    what he's doing?

6.   "It landed at the bottom of the stairs in a heap."
      Are you shocked by how they treat the body?

7.   "If someone sees us, they see us. If they don't, they don't."
      Are you worried that they might get caught?

8.   "Calm down. There's no need to rush. Put the wipers on."
      Why is Alex so panicky?

9.   How does Martyn hope to spend Christmas day?

10.   There is a tense atmosphere during the car journey.
      Why is it so tense?

11.   What do they need the rocks for?

12.   "The cold, the dark, the danger – it didn't matter"
      Why isn't Martyn worried or scared?

13.   "We'd done it." Has their plan gone well?

14.   "Who did I hurt? I hurt nobody." In your opinion, has
      Martyn done anything wrong?

15.   Why does Martyn ask Alex about Dean?

16.   "He's not going to get the money, though, is he?"
      What do you think will happen next?

Chapter Five, Sunday

Questions

1.   How well has Martyn adjusted to living alone?

2.   "And the telephone, mute and black, still waiting. Go on,
      before it's too late. It was too late."
      Do you think Martyn is one hundred per cent happy with
      how things with the body have gone?
      Is it too late now for him to change his mind and go to the
      police?

3.   "I hate that. Not knowing where someone is. It bothers
      me."
      Is Martyn a very possessive friend?

4.   "You wait all day for something, then when it finally
      comes you wish you hadn't bothered."
      Does Martyn depend on Alex too much or is he just very
      lonely?

Chapter Six, Monday

Questions

1. "I whistled into the bathroom and whistled as I whistled."
    Are you surprised by how cheerful Martyn is here?
    Has he gotten over his father's death very quickly, or is it
    fair enough considering how his father treated him?

2. "It left me cold. Ashamed. Scared. Dirty and bad. But at
    the same time I felt something else, too."
    What does this tell you about Martyn?

3. "I just needed some time away from it."
    Do you think Alex is coping well with the events of the
    last few days?

4. "Don't be stupid."
    Is Alex right to make Martyn wait another day
    before they start spending the money?

5. "'Thanks, Alex,' I said. 'For everything.'"
    Is Alex a good friend?

6.   "I'm glad to see the back of her."
       Describe Dean's personality.

7.   "You're not getting any money."
       Is Martyn brave here?

8.   "I had him. He couldn't afford not to believe it."
       Has Martyn's plan gone well?

9.   How does Alex help Martyn get the better of Dean?

10.   "I was weightless. Floating."
       Why might Martyn feel this way?

11.   "All that's left is me and Alex. And thirty thousand
       pounds."
       What would you do next if you were Martyn?
       What do you think he'll do next?

12.   "There was a glazed look in her eyes, distant, not-quite-
       there."
       Why is Alex behaving so strangely, in your opinion?

13.   "Everything had worked. I felt good inside."
       Has Martyn thought of everything?

14.   "If she wanted to spend the money on presents, clothes,
       that kind of stuff...well, that was fine."
       Is Martyn a good friend to Alex?

15. "'Let's talk about it tomorrow,' she said eventually."
    Did you ever think Alex would run away with Martyn?
    Explain your answer.

16. "That was the last time I ever saw her." Explain your reaction to this line.

Chapter Seven, Tuesday

Questions

1. "No answer. I waited some more, pacing up and down, looking at the clock every two minutes."
    We've never seen Martyn so agitated and edgy. Explain his behaviour as he waits for Alex to turn up.

2. What has Alex done?

3. "Used you. Betrayed you. It was all an act."
    Do you feel sorry for Martyn here?

4. "Why were they asking about Dean? I couldn't work out what to say, whether to lie or just say nothing."
    How would you feel, if you were Martyn?

5. What has Alex done to Dean?

6. "It was too much."
    Can you believe that Alex has done all of this?

7. "They'd thought of everything."
    Has Alex's plan gone well?
    Do you feel sorry for Martyn here?

8.   Did you expect something like this to happen in the story?

Chapter Eight, Christmas Day

Questions

1. "Do what you'd do if you were innocent."
   Do you think Martyn acts convincingly here?

2. Does Detective Inspector Breece, the police officer, treat Martyn fairly?

3. "I sat there on the edge of the bed and blubbed like a baby."
   Why is Martyn breaking down in tears, in your opinion?

4. "I didn't understand how it had all got so complicated."
   Do you think Martyn will get caught?

5. Do you think the story Martyn makes up about Dean will get him off the hook?

6. "He knew I was lying."
   What would you do next if you were Martyn?

7. How did the police find the body?

8. What is Alex trying to do now, in your opinion?

Chapter Nine, Epilogue

Questions

1. "I've been at Aunty Jean's for almost a year now."
   Does this ending surprise you?

2. What is it like for him, living with his aunt?

3. Why couldn't the police solve the case? Mention each problem they encountered.

4. What is your reaction to Alex's letter?

5. What did you like and dislike about the story's ending?

Follow Up Questions

Questions

1. Although Martyn is not always a nice character, he is an interesting character. What makes him interesting?

2. Questions of right and wrong occur frequently in this story. Should Martyn have been punished for what he did, or are you happy with how the story ended?

3. Did you misjudge Alex? Should we have realised sooner what she was up to?

4. Did you enjoy this story?
    What did you like and dislike about it?

Visit www.scenebysceneguides.com to see our full catalogue of
Classroom Questions and Workbooks.

Hamlet Scene by Scene Classroom Questions

Romeo and Juliet Scene by Scene Classroom Questions

King Lear Scene by Scene Classroom Questions

Macbeth Scene by Scene Classroom Questions

A Doll's House Classroom Questions

Animal Farm Classroom Questions

Foster Classroom Questions

Good Night, Mr. Tom Classroom Questions

Subscribe to our newsletter at www.scenebysceneguides.com/newsletter to keep up to date with all the latest title releases

Martyn Pig Classroom Questions

Of Mice and Men Classroom Questions

Pride and Prejudice Classroom Questions

Private Peaceful Classroom Questions

The Fault in Our Stars Classroom Questions

The Old Man and the Sea Classroom Questions

The Outsiders Classroom Questions

To Kill a Mockingbird Classroom Questions

The Spinning Heart Classroom Questions

32993915R00018

Printed in Great Britain
by Amazon